First World War
and Army of Occupation
War Diary
France, Belgium and Germany

1 INDIAN CAVALRY DIVISION
Headquarters, Branches and Services
Royal Army Ordnance Corps
Deputy Assistant Director Ordnance Services
9 November 1914 - 30 December 1916

WO95/1169/2

The Naval & Military Press Ltd
www.nmarchive.com
Published in association with The National Archives

Published by

The Naval & Military Press Ltd

Unit 10 Ridgewood Industrial Park,

Uckfield, East Sussex,

TN22 5QE England

Tel: +44 (0) 1825 749494

www.naval-military-press.com

www.nmarchive.com

This diary has been reprinted in facsimile from the original. Any imperfections are inevitably reproduced and the quality may fall short of modern type and cartographic standards.

© **Crown Copyright**
Images reproduced by permission of The National Archives, London, England, 2015.

Contents

Document type	Place/Title	Date From	Date To
Heading	WO95/1169/2		
Heading	1 Ind Cav Div D.A.D.O.S. 1914 Nov-1916 Dec		
Heading	War Diary of D.A.D.O.S. 1st Indian Cavalry Division. From 9th November 1914 To 30th June 1915		
Heading	War Diary of Captain A. F. N. Barron R.A. DADOS. 1st Ind. Cavy. Division From 9.11.14. To 31-12-14 Volume I		
War Diary	Marseilles	09/11/1914	14/11/1914
War Diary	Orleans	17/11/1914	20/11/1914
War Diary	Lozinghem	30/11/1914	11/12/1914
War Diary	Lillers	12/12/1914	22/12/1914
War Diary	Berguette	23/12/1914	26/12/1914
War Diary	Aire	28/12/1914	31/12/1914
Heading	War Diary of Captain A.F.N. Barron R.A. DADOS 1st Ind. Cav. Divn. From 1.1.15 To 31.1.15. Vol. I.		
War Diary	Aire	01/01/1915	31/01/1915
Heading	War Diary of Captain A.F.N. Barron. R.A. DADOS. 1st Ind. Cav. Divn. From 1.2.15. To 28.2.15. Vol I.		
War Diary	Aire	01/02/1915	18/02/1915
War Diary	War Diary of Major. A.F.N. Barron R.A. DADOS 1st Ind. Cav. Divn. From 1.3.15. To 31.3.15. Vol I.		
War Diary	Aire	09/03/1915	26/03/1915
Heading	War Diary of Major AFN Barron RA DADOS 1st Ind Cav Divn. From 1.4.15. to 30.4.15. vol I		
War Diary	Aire	17/04/1915	27/04/1915
Heading	War Diary of Major A.F.N. Barron RA. DADOS 1st MD Cav Divn		
War Diary	Aire	02/05/1915	30/05/1915
Heading	War Diary of Major AFN Barron RA DADOS 1st Ind Cav Divn From 1.6.15 To 30-6-15		
War Diary	Aire	04/06/1915	11/06/1915
Heading	War Diary of D.A.D.O.S. 1st Indian Cavalry Division From 1st July 1915 To 31st July 1915		
War Diary	Aire	16/07/1915	31/07/1915
Heading	War Diary of D.A.D.O.S. 1st Indian Cavalry Division From 1st August 1915 To 31st August 1915		
War Diary	Aire Sur Lys	01/08/1915	07/08/1915
Heading	War Diary of D.A.D.O.S. 1st Indian Cavalry Division From 1st September 1915 To 30th September 1915.		
War Diary		01/09/1915	24/09/1915
Heading	War Diary of D.A.D.O.S. 1st Indian Cavalry Division From 23rd October 1915 To 28th October 1915.		
War Diary	Longpre C.G.S.	23/10/1915	28/10/1915
Heading	War Diary of D.A.D.O.S. 1st Indian Cavalry Division. From 6th November 1915 To 30th November 1915		
War Diary	Longpre	06/11/1915	25/11/1915
Heading	War Diary of D.A.D.O.S. 1st Indian Cavalry Division From 1st December 1915 To 31st December 1915.		
Heading	Major A.F.N. Barron Ra. I.O.D. Dad Of 1st Ind. Cav. Div.		

War Diary	Longpre	01/12/1915	23/12/1915
Heading	War Diary of D.A.D.O.S. 1st India Cavalry Division From 1st January 1916 To 31st January 1916.		
War Diary	Bouttencourt	20/01/1916	27/01/1916
Heading	War Diary of D.A.D.O.S. 1st Indian Cavalry Division From 1st March 1916 To 31st March 1916.		
War Diary	Dargnies	05/03/1916	24/03/1916
War Diary	Auxi-Le-Chateau	25/03/1916	27/03/1916
Heading	War Diary of D.A.D.O.S. 1st Indian Cavalry Division From 1st April 1916 To 20th April 1916.		
War Diary	Auxi-Le-Chateau	01/04/1916	01/04/1916
War Diary	Wail	02/04/1916	25/04/1916
War Diary	Yvrench	27/04/1916	30/04/1916
Heading	War Diary of D.A.D.O.S. 1st Indian Cavalry Division From 1st May 1916 To 31st May 1916.		
War Diary	Yvrench	01/05/1916	01/05/1916
War Diary	Wail	06/05/1916	07/05/1916
War Diary	Le Cauroy	09/05/1916	26/05/1916
War Diary	Yvrench	01/05/1916	01/05/1916
War Diary	Wail	06/05/1916	07/05/1916
War Diary	Le Cauroy	09/05/1916	26/05/1916
Heading	War Diary of D.A.D.O.S. 1st Indian Cavalry Division From 1st June 1916 To 30th June 1916		
War Diary	Le Cauroy	03/06/1916	30/06/1916
Heading	War Diary of D.A.D.O.S. 1st Indian Cavalry Division From 1st July 1916 To 31st July 1916.		
War Diary	Auxi-Le-Chateau	02/07/1916	17/07/1916
War Diary	Villers-Chatel	19/07/1916	29/08/1916
Heading	War Diary of D.A.D.O.S. 1st Indian Cavalry Division From 1st September 1916 To 30th September 1916.		
War Diary	Villers Chatel	01/09/1916	02/09/1916
War Diary	Frohen le Grand	03/09/1916	03/09/1916
War Diary	St Ricquier	04/09/1916	09/09/1916
War Diary	Doullens	11/09/1916	12/09/1916
War Diary	Allonville	13/09/1916	15/09/1916
War Diary	Albert	16/09/1916	28/09/1916
War Diary	Ailly-Le-Haut-Clocher	29/09/1916	29/09/1916
War Diary	Ligescourt	30/09/1916	30/09/1916
Heading	War Diary of D.A.D.O.S. 4th Cavalry Division (Late 1st I.B. Division) From 1st October 1916 To 30th November 1916		
War Diary	Ligescourt	01/10/1916	30/10/1916
Heading	War Diary of D.A.D.O.S. 4th Cavy Division Nov. 1st To 30th, 1916		
War Diary	Sivalery-Sur-Somme	02/11/1916	30/11/1916
Heading	War Diary of D.A.D.O.S. 4th Cavalry Division From 1st December 1916 To 31st December 1916		
War Diary	St Valery-Sur-Somme	04/12/1916	30/12/1916

WO 95/1169/2

1 IND CAV DIV

SOTAC

1914 NOV — 1916 DEC

Serial No. 304.

12/1650²

WAR DIARY
OF

D.A.D.O.S., 1st Indian Cavalry Division.

From 9th November 1914 to 30th June 1915.

Army Form C. 2118

WAR DIARY
or
INTELLIGENCE SUMMARY.
(Erase heading not required.)

Dec/14

Confidential

War Diary
of
Captain
Lieut. G.J.N. Barron. R.A. DADOS.
1st Ind: Cav. Divn:

From 9.10.14. To. 31-12.14

Volume I

Army Form C. 2118.

WAR DIARY
or
INTELLIGENCE SUMMARY.

(Erase heading not required.)

Instructions regarding War Diaries and Intelligence Summaries are contained in F.S. Regs., Part II, and the Staff Manual respectively. Title pages will be prepared in manuscript.

Hour, Date, Place.	Summary of Events and Information.	Remarks and references to Appendices
9-11-14. MARSEILLES	Saw the following:— Staff Captain R.A. U Batt. R.H.A. 17th Lancers 6th Cavalry 9th Hodson's Horse 36th Jacob's Horse. And explained re sending in Govt. and private kits, issue of warm clothing, issue of messed scales and new equipt. (moncation, capes and gloves for M. Guns, dial sight no 1, fuze indicator, and telephones and earphones)	And [signature]
11.11.14. MARSEILLES	Saw the following:— R.H.A Brigades Staff. A. Batty. RHA Q. Batty. RHA C. Am Col. RHA G. Am Col. RHA B. Am Col. RHA. 8th Hussars 19th Lancers 30th Lancers Signal Squadron 138 Cavy. Fd. Ambulance	[signature]

Army Form C. 2118.

WAR DIARY
or
INTELLIGENCE SUMMARY.

(Erase heading not required.)

Instructions regarding War Diaries and Intelligence Summaries are contained in F. S. Regs., Part II, and the Staff Manual respectively. Title pages will be prepared in manuscript.

Hour, Date, Place.	Summary of Events and Information.	Remarks and references to Appendices
14.11.14 MARSEILLES	From 7.11.14 (date of arrival of 1st Inds. Cav. Divn.) to this date 2 exchanged all Mk VI .303 used for Mk VII. 3 musketry instructors of Indian manufacture for Lee Enfield. Inspected all machine guns and rifles (the former for exchange and the latter for shortening at ORLEANS). 5 were armed with drum stopping. French interpreters were enlisted and supplied according to the several regts were attached to.	[signature] 14/11/14
	Left by Exp. train at 7 pm for ORLEANS accompanied by Staff Sergt. ROLFE, AOD and Pte WHITE AOC	
17.11.14 ORLEANS	Arrived 12 mid night 16 & 17 at ORLEANS. Visited Camp LEGROUE 33rd Ind. Cav. Bde. found all satisfactory and clear as to ammn. & incurred stores. Could not obtain items of M.G. equipt. asked for by CO ORLEANS. Visited Ordnance depot LA CHAPELLE.	[signature] 7/11

Army Form C. 2118.

WAR DIARY
or
INTELLIGENCE SUMMARY.
(Erase heading not required.)

Hour, Date, Place.	Summary of Events and Information.	Remarks and references to Appendices
18.11.14 ORLEANS	Visited Camps LA SOURCE, 2nd & 8th Cavy Bdes all unfit satisfied and clear about ammy reserve stores. Could not obtain H.G. Equipt required by COO ORLEANS - obtained and gave him Set of "10th Hussars" Equipt - Sub. Condr. V.N. Strickland IOD joined	Rale Ord. ORLEANS M. 402 df 15.11.14 O. 741 df 15.11.14
19.11.14 ORLEANS	Called for return of no. of Black G coats in possession Cavy units (non divn orders) Also trunks on officers trunk to be sold to Govt. Staff Sergt. DEARNLEY. AOC. Pte. WOLSTEN HOLME AOE & ENERAND joined	M.402 df 16.11.14 [signature] 20/11/14
20.11.14 ORLEANS	Staff Sergt. ROLFE to ORD BASE ORLEANS in place of Staff Sergt. DEARNLEY.	

Army Form C. 2118.

WAR DIARY
or
INTELLIGENCE SUMMARY.
(Erase heading not required.)

Hour, Date, Place.	Summary of Events and Information.	Remarks and references to Appendices
30th Nov. 1914 ROZINGHEM.	Arrived here via ABBEVILLE and STOMER, at former reported to D.D.O.S (Lieut General Parsons) at latter to D.D.O.S. G.H.Q. (Col. MATHIEU) DDOS gave instructions re Supply and Ammunition Railheads and new system of issues from Base in bulk of clothing and Munition for which there is a constant demand from HAVRE	
8th Dec.	Truck No 193889 with first consignment of bulk stores arrived at CHOQUES, railhead for Indian Army Corps - Sent to FOUQUEREVIL, railhead, but I car short here in marginal journal. Two more trucks with bulk stores from Base HAVRE. Insuitable to distribute owing to railhead return to LILLERS.	✠ L Cpl Saunders Pte Smith " Jones " Carpenter
9th Dec.		
10th Dec.	Distributed home stores for winter use to AMBALLA and SIRHOTE Brigades in 4 motor lorries. Stokesmen not found owing to change of billetting area not communicated.	
11th Dec.	2 more trucks with bulk stores from base and issue from stores which came 9th distributed in 6 lorries. So lorries returned true with bulk stores from base for units arrived LILLERS. Stokesmen not found.	[signature] 11/12/14

Army Form C. 2118.

WAR DIARY
or
INTELLIGENCE SUMMARY.
(Erase heading not required.)

Instructions regarding War Diaries and Intelligence Summaries are contained in F. S. Regs., Part II, and the Staff Manual respectively. Title pages will be prepared in manuscript.

Hour, Date, Place.	Summary of Events and Information.	Remarks and references to Appendices
LILLERS. 12th Dec. 1914	Moved here, Railhead, from head quarters of the division, as I think it will be wiser for me to see to the distribution of stores & with Rail letter are getting not reliably in the firing line	
LILLERS 20th Dec. 1914	UMBALLA and SIALKOTE Cavy brigades ordered to support Indian Corps	
LILLERS 21st Dec 1914	Returned here to above brigades and their indisposition except to Jodhpur Horse who cover to take delivery.	
LILLERS 22nd Dec 1914	After 10 days trial I am of an opinion that this is at railhead - then he can see to the distribution of Ordnance stores better than in any other place. With a motor at his disposal he can easily keep in touch with the divisional and brigade staffs	Railhead the place for stores when troops in trenches. [signature] 31/12/14

Army Form C. 2118.

WAR DIARY
or
INTELLIGENCE SUMMARY.

(Erase heading not required.)

Hour, Date, Place.	Summary of Events and Information.	Remarks and references to Appendices
BERGUETTE 23rd Nov 1914	Rail head changed here this morning - Hd Qrs of Stn from LOZINGHEM to BOURECQ. Cavalry Corps Hd Qrs formed and moved to ST QUENTIN from about 5, Corps about 7 miles from railhead. Received large supply of horse shoes - up to now the supply has been bad, shoes wearout quickly and drop off easily in inky weather. Shoes are arriving with only about 2 's fitted with cogs. The ordinary frostnails the latter are not nearly so efficient as the former - Hd find Cavalry Horses take 2's 3's and a small $\frac{4}{p}$ of 4's. Artillery $\frac{4}{p}$ 5's 6's and a few 7's draught horses 9's -10's and 11's to 12's drillers of Cavalry in frosty weather being formed.	Supply of and sizes of horse shoes. Appl 3/12/14

Army Form C. 2118.

WAR DIARY
or
INTELLIGENCE SUMMARY.
(Erase heading not required.)

Instructions regarding War Diaries and Intelligence Summaries are contained in F. S. Regs., Part II, and the Staff Manual respectively. Title pages will be prepared in manuscript.

Hour, Date, Place.	Summary of Events and Information.	Remarks and references to Appendices
BERGUETTE. 26th Dec. 1914	Went to GHQ 2nd Car Corps and consulted QMG re kits for officers — Said I would sell to officers probable consignments.	
AIRE. 28th Dec. 1914.	Arrived from BERGUETTE in morn of rail head	
29th Dec 1914.	To G H Q 15 8th new Car in place of No 1647 with snouted springs to PARIS. Car received No 1882. Spare tools in duty 16-20 Souterenne tracks	
30th Dec 1914	To GHQ interviewed GASTON-SOUILLANT 124 Rue de CALAIS re supply of laundry baskets. He promises to supply up to 8000 at Frs 9 (Esson) per doz, and Frs 9 per doz; superior quality.	
31st Dec 1914.	Return to rail head. Caught dispatch of coal account to B/H if Clearing House Base	[signature] 31/12/14

Gulab Singh & Sons, Calcutta—No. 22 Army C. B.H.C—1,07,00.

Army Form C. 2118.

Jan 15

WAR DIARY
or
INTELLIGENCE SUMMARY.
(Erase heading not required.)

Instructions regarding War Diaries and Intelligence Summaries are contained in F.S. Regs., Part II and the Staff Manual respectively. Title pages will be prepared in manuscript.

Hour, Date, Place	Summary of Events and Information	Remarks and references to Appendices
Preserved	Confidential War Diary of Captain. A.F.N. BARRON. R.A. DADOS 1st Ind: Cav: Divⁿ From 1.1.15 To 31.1.15. Vol. I.	

WAR DIARY
or
INTELLIGENCE SUMMARY.
(Erase heading not required.)

Army Form C. 2118.

Hour, Date, Place		Summary of Events and Information	Remarks and references to Appendices
AIRE.			
January '15	1.	Condr. McLAURIN and Sub Condr. WHITEHEAD I.O.D. joined my staff and posted as remount officers of SIALKOTE and AMBALA Cav: Bdes respectively	
	5.	Visited units of the division paying bills for shoeing horses. These bills have been incurred on account of the supply of shoes being inadequate	
	6.	Since the advanced ordnance depot at LE MANS has been amalgamated with the base at LE HAVRE the supply of stores has much improved	
	18th	DDOS GHQ has called for a report on the matter of horse shoes, the short supply of which has seriously affected the Ind Cav Corps. Report submitted showing all issues, outstanding, and demands from base	
	19.	Interviewed DOS at GHQ re shortage of horse shoes. DAQMG 1st Cav: Divn also seen there and reported same difficulty. Result, DOS send trace to send up shoes at once	[signature] 18/1

(73989) W4141—463. 400,000. 9/14. H.&J.Ltd. Forms/C. 2118/10.

Army Form C. 2118.

WAR DIARY
or
INTELLIGENCE SUMMARY.
(Erase heading not required.)

Hour, Date, Place	Summary of Events and Information	Remarks and references to Appendices
AIRE.		
January 21.	QMG Expeditionary force visited Railhead. Brought the matter of shortage of horse shoes to his notice and told him that shoes were coming up from base satisfactorily	
26.	Since 23rd some 8400 sets of horse shoes have been received from base, this has put the supply on a satisfactory basis for the present. Experience shows that every horse requires shoeing at least once in 3 weeks or roughly 10,000 sets are required monthly for a cavalry division	
30.	The divisional artillery moved out to join 28th division. Informed brigades 28th Divn, DADOS GHQ, Base and regulating station. At midnight 30-31 orders received to be ready to move in two hours, ordnance ready 1·30 am 31st.	

Army Form C. 2118.

WAR DIARY
or
INTELLIGENCE SUMMARY.
(Erase heading not required.)

(3)

Instructions regarding War Diaries and Intelligence Summaries are contained in F.S. Regs., Part II. and the Staff Manual respectively. Title pages will be prepared in manuscript.

Hour, Date, Place	Summary of Events and Information	Remarks and references to Appendices
AIRE. January 31	I took out a lorry full of stores for the R.H.A. to STRAZEELE. Had to go personally as their position was doubtful. Daoos nearly always to informed of units position by G.S.	And /s/

Army Form C. 2118.

WAR DIARY
or
INTELLIGENCE SUMMARY.
(Erase heading not required.)

Feb. '15

Confidential

War Diary
of
Captain A.F.N. BARRON. R.A. DADOS.
1st Ind: Cav: Divn:

From 1.2.15   To 28.2.15

Vol I

Army Form C. 2118.

WAR DIARY
or
INTELLIGENCE SUMMARY.
(Erase heading not required.)

Instructions regarding War Diaries and Intelligence Summaries are contained in F.S. Regs., Part II. and the Staff Manual respectively. Title pages will be prepared in manuscript.

Hour, Date, Place	Summary of Events and Information	Remarks and references to Appendices
AIRE February 1	Lt Col. E.P. CARTER R.A. took over duties of ADDS 2nd Corps and Capt. KERWICK. IOD came to 2nd. Officer Corps troops - I handed over these duties.	
5.	Payment issues to officers from bulk supplies sanctioned. Their always done this measure where the name was absolutely necessary	SOS A 2743 of 22.1.15
7.	Pattern of rifle cover, approved by GOC, sent to OSTS. GHQ be called for - The covers are necessary to protect the breech mechanism of rifles during wet and muddy weather - The best device is an old sock with toe cut off. DDOS GHQ informed me that cartridges newly made of rifles were safe but not sighted for lute VII cartridges.	SOS 9/1/36 of 31.1.15

Army Form C. 2118.

WAR DIARY
or
INTELLIGENCE SUMMARY.
(Erase heading not required.)

Hour, Date, Place	Summary of Events and Information	Remarks and references to Appendices
AIRE February 15.	To BOMY with ASDS and AAP and 1st Ind Div Gen to settle dispute between myself and 9th Hussars Horse about issue of nose bags and boots. It was agreed that unit had received all indication for which must mark off receipts on their copy of indent of Wty wish to know what stores are due to them.	S.O.S. wire OA 2532 4/15/215
18.	New system of demand from base of stores wanted in bulk. The system is that stores will submit a list each week of what stores he actually has due to truck. The base will send up each class of stores on separate days. The great advantage of this system seems to be that stores will not be looked up in the railway while travelling to & from troops so much as under the system an average quantity are sent to each D.A.D.O.S who very frequently did not require the kit & had to return to base	Anvil 15/2

Army Form C. 2118.

March /15

WAR DIARY
or
INTELLIGENCE SUMMARY.
(Erase heading not required.)

Instructions regarding War Diaries and Intelligence Summaries are contained in F. S. Regs., Part II, and the Staff Manual respectively. Title pages will be prepared in manuscript.

Hour, Date, Place.	Summary of Events and Information.	Remarks and references to Appendices.
Original	Confidential War Diary of Major. A.F.N. BARRON. R.A. DADOS 1st Ind Cav: Bim From 1.3.15 To. 31.3.15 Vol I.	

Army Form C. 2118.

WAR DIARY
or
INTELLIGENCE SUMMARY.
(Erase heading not required.)

Hour, Date, Place.	Summary of Events and Information.	Remarks and references to Appendices.
AIRE March 9.	To ESTAIRES to consult O.C.s 8th Divn to whom the artillery of 1st Ind Cav Divn is now attached.	
11.	The Divn moved into the BOIS des DAMES S.W. of Bethune. Sent out reference stores in supply lorries as the distance from railhead is too great to run the ordnance lorries twice to get round each unit of the respective brigades.	
12.	Went along BETHUNE - LOCON - ESTAIRES road & watched the working of ammunition supply. Inspected M.G. Tripods of 30th Lancers & ordered them to be replaced.	
14.	The Division moved from billets in the BOIS des DAMES	
15.	To billets in BOURECQ - AMETTES - St HILAIRES - FERVIN	
	DoS orders that Indian units will make their own arrangements for supply of bodyes as these are not forwarded in England	OSG 3602/245 d/10.3.15 And 7/3.

Gulab Singh & Sons, Calcutta—No. 22 Army Q—5-8-14—1,07,000.

Army Form C. 2118.

WAR DIARY
or
INTELLIGENCE SUMMARY.
(Erase heading not required.)

Instructions regarding War Diaries and Intelligence Summaries are contained in F. S. Regs., Part II, and the Staff Manual respectively. Title pages will be prepared in manuscript.

Hour, Date, Place.	Summary of Events and Information.	Remarks and references to Appendices.
AIRE		
March 21.	Received decision from DDVS that it has been decided to introduce brood-mares for all services, collars draught having been found unsuitable.	OSA/3193 d/17.3.15
26.	Orders received from DDVS that winter clothing of horses and men are to be returned to PARIS for cleansing and disinfecting. Clothing to be viewed by boards to decide what is worth retaining, and the remainder to be burnt.	A/3295 d/25.3.15 And 26/3

Gulab Singh & Sons, Calcutta—No. 22 Army C.—5-8-14—1,07,000.

Army Form C. 2118.

WAR DIARY
or
INTELLIGENCE SUMMARY.
(Erase heading not required.)

April '15

Hour, Date, Place.	Summary of Events and Information.	Remarks and references to Appendices.

Confidential

War Diary
of
Major A F N BARRON R.A. DADOS.
1st Ind Cav Bde.

From 1.4.15 to 30.4.15

Vol. I

Army Form C. 2118.

WAR DIARY
or
INTELLIGENCE SUMMARY.
(Erase heading not required.)

Instructions regarding War Diaries and Intelligence Summaries are contained in F. S. Regs., Part II, and the Staff Manual respectively. Title pages will be prepared in manuscript.

Hour, Date, Place.		Summary of Events and Information.	Remarks and references to Appendices.
AIRE.			
April.	17	D.O.S. orders that COO's representative at railhead is to join Railhead Commandant's staff and be under that officer for discipline viz. L.Cpl CARPENTER transferred accordingly	O.S.A/3432 d/11.4.15
	18.	Shield extension pieces are to be provided for QF 13 prs as soon as QF 18 prs has been completed	
		D.O.S reports that his five hair ornaments on the military equipment on horse rugs being sent to PARIS wct. Jean has been very careful that all from 1st Ind Car Divn were handed over to Railhead Commandant duly.	
	20.	A.D.O.S and myself have tested 2 patterns of seatbands to fit all the Futures with Indian Cavalry viz both the Curzed and one the straight Futures	

A.D.
20/4.

Army Form C. 2118.

WAR DIARY
or
INTELLIGENCE SUMMARY.
(Erase heading not required.)

Hour, Date, Place.	Summary of Events and Information.	Remarks and references to Appendices.
AIRE April 2d	This matter of the Indian Cavalry Silladar not fitting in to the government pattern of Tulwar scabbard is one of many incidents which have gone to prove the disadvantage of the Indian Silladar Cavalry system as regards the supply of ordnance stores in the field — Every Indian Cavalry regiment has a different private pattern of most of the more important articles of equipment, many of which cannot be replaced by government pattern. And it is this that has in my experience caused a lot of unnecessary expenditure of money and time — I am of opinion that, however advantageous the Silladar system may be in other ways, as far as the supply of equipment is concerned it has every disadvantage, and in future all cavalry rgts should be fitted throughout with government pattern articles.	

And [signature]

Army Form C. 2118.

WAR DIARY
or
INTELLIGENCE SUMMARY.
(Erase heading not required.)

Instructions regarding War Diaries and Intelligence Summaries are contained in F. S. Regs., Part II, and the Staff Manual respectively. Title pages will be prepared in manuscript.

Hour, Date, Place.		Summary of Events and Information.	Remarks and references to Appendices.
AIRE			
April	24	The Division moved to vicinity of CASSEL	
	27.	The Division moved to WATOU - I sent out advance stores on the supply lorries. RHA batteries returned from 7th Division, OC's complained that shells away from 1st Ind Cav Bde they had had difficulty in getting advance stores. This was probably due to their not standing natural going round the country after them	And 27/4

Army Form C. 2118.

WAR DIARY
or
INTELLIGENCE SUMMARY.
(Erase heading not required.)

May 15

Instructions regarding War Diaries and Intelligence Summaries are contained in F. S. Regs., Part II, and the Staff Manual respectively. Title pages will be prepared in manuscript.

Hour, Date, Place.	Summary of Events and Information.	Remarks and references to Appendices.
	Confidential War Diary of Major A.F.N. BARRON. R.A. DADOS. 1st Ind Cav Divn from 1.5.15 To 31.5.15	

Army Form C. 2118.

WAR DIARY
or
INTELLIGENCE SUMMARY.
(Erase heading not required.)

Instructions regarding War Diaries and Intelligence Summaries are contained in F. S. Regs., Part II, and the Staff Manual respectively. Title pages will be prepared in manuscript.

Hour, Date, Place.	Summary of Events and Information.	Remarks and references to Appendices.
AIRE. May.		
2.	The division returned to AIRE.	
5.	1st KDGs returned a quantity of generator clubs and primers to Richud. These were issued to the Field Squadron for practice purposes.	
17.	The division moved to ALLOUAGNE because stores sent out in supply lorries.	
17.	Orders received to send escorts to base by DRLS and not by telegram as heretofore.	
18.	Sanction received to equip cavalry regiments with 20 bags saddle ammunition to carry reserve ammts. up to date rgts have carried them reserve ammts in various ways, mostly in empty boxes. The English pattern ammtn box has been found to make a very bad pack load.	

Army Form C. 2118.

WAR DIARY
or
INTELLIGENCE SUMMARY.
(Erase heading not required.)

Instructions regarding War Diaries and Intelligence Summaries are contained in F. S. Regs., Part II, and the Staff Manual respectively. Title pages will be prepared in manuscript.

Hour, Date, Place.		Summary of Events and Information.	Remarks and references to Appendices.
AIRE			
May.	21	The division entrained to billets in the vicinity of AIRE	
	22	SoS ordered that incidents should be sent to base made out on proper form (A F G994) — This was suggested by A.O.D.E. Ind Cav Corps some time ago. 1 century old needs to base for storage	OSA 4056 d/20.5.15 Ing. 165/1stCD d/22.5.15
	27.	The division was attached to 2nd Army and marched to STAPLE.	
	28.	The division marched to PURROUCK and from there 300 men per nyts went in buses to VLAMERTINGE	
	30.	A carriage QF 13 pr returned to base, which had been asked for to replace one from U'RPAA by S.O.M.	And. 307/5

Army Form C. 2118.

WAR DIARY
or
INTELLIGENCE SUMMARY.
(Erase heading not required.)

June 15

Instructions regarding War Diaries and Intelligence Summaries are contained in F. S. Regs., Part II, and the Staff Manual respectively. Title pages will be prepared in manuscript.

Hour, Date, Place.	Summary of Events and Information.	Remarks and references to Appendices.
	Confidential War Diary of Major A F N BARON R A Comdg at Mhow Can from from 1.6.15 To 30-6-15.	

by him

Army Form C. 2118.

WAR DIARY
or
INTELLIGENCE SUMMARY.
(Erase heading not required.)

Instructions regarding War Diaries and Intelligence Summaries are contained in F. S. Regs., Part II, and the Staff Manual respectively. Title pages will be prepared in manuscript.

Hour, Date, Place.	Summary of Events and Information.	Remarks and references to Appendices.
AIRE. June '15 4th	40-0 smoke helmets issued, this was enough to give one to every man in the Trenches.	
5th	Issued a horse from the 1st K D Gs. The gun which this is to replace was destroyed by a shell on 2.6.15. Replacement only took 3 days.	
11th	The division moved back into billets in the vicinity of AIRE. Since 28th May the advanced report centre of the division with 300 men of each regt, auth Column, Field troops and Field Squadron has been in the vicinity of VLAMERTINGE about 35 miles from billets at AIRE. The horses and artillery have been at RURROUCK about 20 miles from AIRE and the same distance from VLAMERTINGE	

11/6

Army Form C. 2118.

WAR DIARY
or
INTELLIGENCE SUMMARY.
(Erase heading not required.)

Instructions regarding War Diaries and Intelligence Summaries are contained in F. S. Regs., Part II, and the Staff Manual respectively. Title pages will be prepared in manuscript.

Hour, Date, Place.	Summary of Events and Information.	Remarks and references to Appendices.
AIRE. June 15	To work the supply of ordnance stores to both places I made the following arrangements which worked satisfactorily: One warrant officer (Sub Condr JOHNSON) with advanced position and the other two (Condr McLAURIN and Sub Condr WHITEHEAD) with the troops at the billeting area at RUBROUCK The ordnance lorries went out to each position as necessary hardly two to such. As soon as the troops who had been in the firing line returned it was discovered that they had been attacked by lice. This necessitated giving them a complete change of under clothing. The old clothes that were worth it were mended washed and disinfected and used to meet ordinary demands	Apps 1/6

Gulab Singh & Sons, Calcutta—No. 22 Army C.—5-8-14—1,07,000.

Serial No. 304.

121/6502

WAR DIARY
OF
D.A.D.O.S. 1st Indian Cavalry Division.

FROM 1st July 1915. TO 31st July 1915.

Army Form C. 2118.

WAR DIARY
or
INTELLIGENCE SUMMARY.
(Erase heading not required.)

Instructions regarding War Diaries and Intelligence Summaries are contained in F. S. Regs., Part II, and the Staff Manual respectively. Title pages will be prepared in manuscript.

Hour, Date, Place.	Summary of Events and Information.	Remarks and references to Appendices.
AIRE.		
16th July 16.	Drew from ammunition outhouse 1st Army. ST VENANT Grenades for practice	
18	Condr HOCKNEY took over chief clerk from Condr STRICKLAND	
20.	Visited machine gun school GHQ to inspect McCONNEL carrying experts, withdrew 38 rifles from each of the RHA batteries	
29.	Major ROOKE AOD joined & took over duties	
31.	Handed my duties over to Major Rooke –	

Serial No 304.

12/16958

WAR DIARY
OF

D.A.D.O.S., 1st Indian Cavalry Division.

From 1st August 1915 TO 31st August 1915.

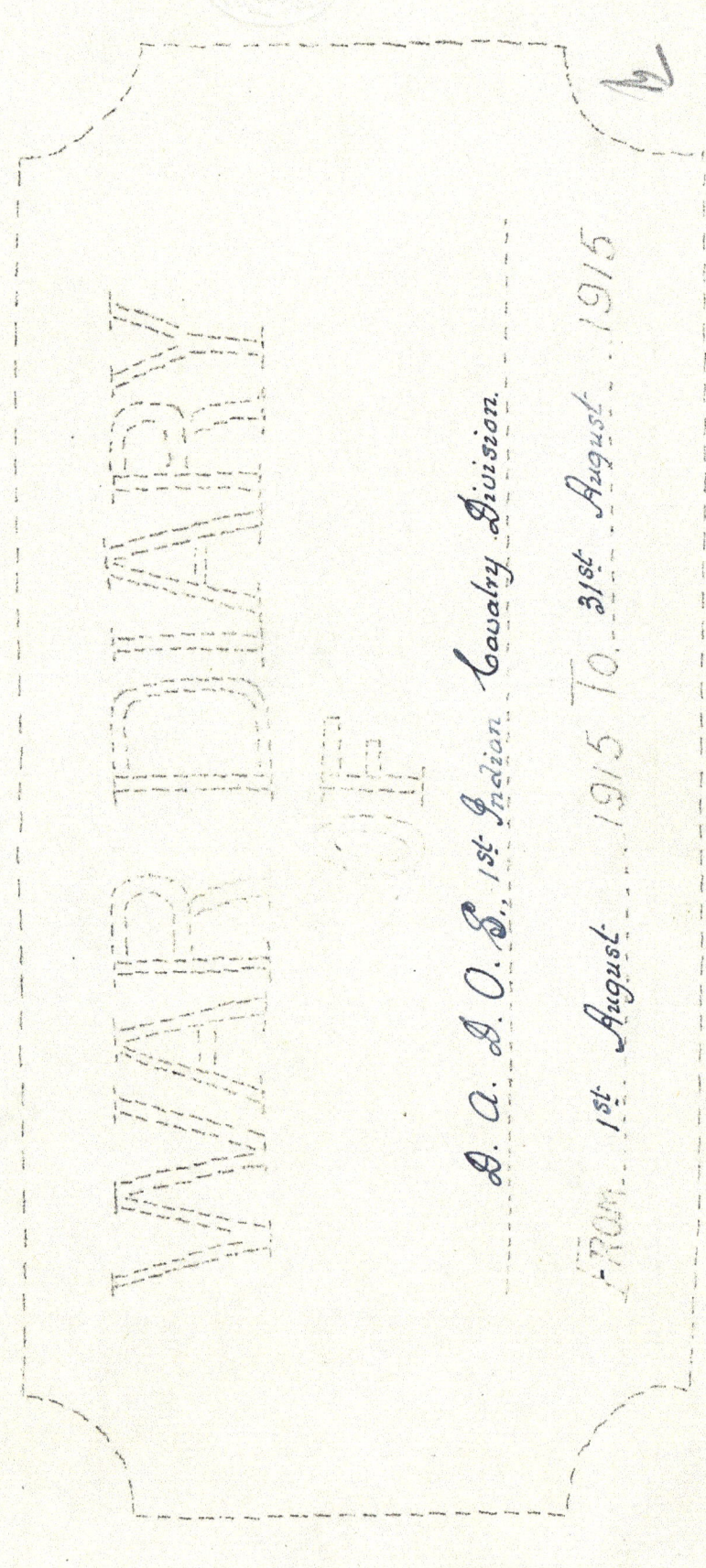

WAR DIARY
or
INTELLIGENCE SUMMARY.
(Erase heading not required.)

Army Form C. 2118

Hour, Date, Place.	Summary of Events and Information.	Remarks and references to Appendices.
AIRES sur LYS. 1.8.15.	Major B.P.S. Roper A.O.D. took over duties of D.A.D.O.S. This Division	
2.8.15.	The 5th Lsr the area and proceeded by march to area taken up by between LONGPRÉ and DOMART. Railway ~~Longpré~~ 5 lorries were placed at the disposal of the D.O.D. for conveyance of Stores personnel etc. of these, 2 carrying horseshoes, clothing etc moved into the 2 echelons of the supply col; with a view to making small issues of these necessary amounts. The arrangement is one where an indent was not satisfactory as it was not clear to me that it was necessary in so short a march. Some units where Staffs appear to be deficient in intelligence complained about this order not put forward, but it appears on enquiring they had not made their requirements known to anyone.	

420
1-9-15
D.A.D.O.S.
1st INDIAN CAVALRY DIVISION

Hour, Date, Place.	Summary of Events and Information.	Remarks and references to Appendices.
7.6.15 **B**	Major Renshaw took over the duties of D.A.D.O.S. of the 2 W.M. Cav Bde during temporary absence of Major Dickens R.A. with the Bt. Pr. The Sub Distr. Bt. went forward and acted as reserve to 2nd Bde who occupied trenches. This led to an alteration in the system of drawing Ordnance Stores. Stores for this extent both were sent out by the Supply Col: daily to a Refilling Pt where Brigade Transport took them on to units. The same method previously exists when this relieved the 2nd Bde in the Trenches. Indents for stores required in the Trenches were made up and the stores sent on a lorry. All other indents were completed to the Regt N Qr in the Willerton area.	

Army Form C.2

WAR DIARY
or
INTELLIGENCE SUMMARY.
(Erase heading not required.)

Instructions regarding War Diaries and Intelligence Summaries are contained in F. S. Regs., Part II, and the Staff Manual respectively. Title pages will be prepared in manuscript.

Hour, Date, Place.	Summary of Events and Information.	Remarks and references to Appendices.

During the month arrangements were commenced for fitting out a Bathing Establishment at S.O.E.14 where men could bathe and receive clean clothing on coming out of the Trenches. These arrangements are not in a sufficiently advanced state to enable me to express any further opinion as to satisfactory. The arrangement as carried out by a Medl Offr under the O.C. 9th 81st and a surveillance exercised over punctures by the [illegible]

1/9/15

B.T. Rutherford A.D.M.S
Major McCarthy

Serial No. 304.

121/7286

Confidential

War Diary

of

D.A.D.O.S. 1st Indian Cavalry Division.

FROM 1st September 1915. TO 30th September 1915.

Army Form C. 2118.

WAR DIARY
of
INTELLIGENCE SUMMARY.
(Erase heading not required.)

Instructions regarding War Diaries and Intelligence Summaries are contained in F. S. Regs., Part II, and the Staff Manual respectively. Title pages will be prepared in manuscript.

Hour, Date, Place.	Summary of Events and Information.	Remarks and references to Appendices.
1.9.15.	The Bathing Establishment came into being the month but had hardly got into working order when on the 22nd orders were received to move and change Rearward.	during
22.9.15.	The B₂ moved into the new billetting area at DOULLENS.	
24.9.15.	The Rearhead at Hq LONGPRÉ was closed and reference at DOULLENS at 6 a.m. Issues were not made while the B.H.S was on the move. This is regrettable, as it would have furnished useful practice but units are surrendering to cover any but adequately regimental stores within or thereabouts. It was decided to discontinue the army without ear-practical scheme of daily issuing of thereabouts. I had never been in favour of this scheme as I consider it hardly possible to carry out an	

Serial No. 304.

Confidential

12/7601

War Diary

of

A.A. & Q.S., 1st Indian Cavalry Division.

FROM 23rd October 1915) TO 28th October 1915.
         1st   31st

Army Form C. 2118.

WAR DIARY
or
INTELLIGENCE SUMMARY.
(Erase heading not required.)

Hour, Date, Place.	Summary of Events and Information.	Remarks and references to Appendices.
LONGPRÉ lè S. 23.10.15.	Railhead moved from DOULLENS to LONGPRE. The march of October has been, from an Ordnance point of view, without incident worth recording. The S.O.O. and workshops is organised so that ordnance stores are immediately available when needed. No requisitions for ordnance stores up to now, neither has there been any charge being necessary.	
28.10.15.	Lieut A.T. Sheed A.O.D. joined for a course of instruction in Divisional duties.	D.A.D. Ross may A.O.D. Ser-Sgt. 1st The Car 45

6.11.15

WAR DIARY
or
INTELLIGENCE SUMMARY.

(Erase heading not required.)

Army Form C. 2118.

Instructions regarding War Diaries and Intelligence Summaries are contained in F.S. Regs., Part II, and the Staff Manual respectively. Title pages will be prepared in manuscript.

Hour, Date, Place.	Summary of Events and Information.	Remarks and references to Appendices.
	undertaking to deliver horseshoes daily, and the scheme seems to work, units tis is independent. In future units will submit indents to me for office on Fridays for shoes for the week next but one. These will be issued bi-weekly on Sundays + Fridays was visit consisting up to 15 days supply from the Ordnance deposits on these days. This seems to the worst one thing that the Army + Hence the res- ponsibility of estimating requirements on units, we alone are in a position to do so accurately. The Bathing Establishment has found to be too remote from the bill Mary area was closed and Sun detailed towing token into use by the 1/ Ind Cav Bd. 3.10.15	B.H. Rooke Brig M.G. S.N.C.D. 1 Ind Car Bgd

Serial No. 304

744/12/080

Confidential

Diary

of

S.S.O., 1st Indian Cavalry Division.

FROM 1st/6th November 1915 TO 30th November 1915

Army Form C. 2118.

WAR DIARY

or

INTELLIGENCE SUMMARY.

(Erase heading not required.)

Instructions regarding War Diaries and Intelligence Summaries are contained in F. S. Regs., Part II, and the Staff Manual respectively. Title pages will be prepared in manuscript.

Hour, Date, Place.	Summary of Events and Information.	Remarks and references to Appendices.
LONGPRÉ		
6.11.15.	I took over duties of P.A.D.O.S. 1st & 2nd Cav. Divn from Major B.P.S. ROOKE. A.O.D.	Ard
22.11.15.	21 Pumps purchased by C.O. of this division, for the purpose of drawing water from streams to troughs.	Ard
23.11.15.	415 lanterns tent folding in addition to authorised scale (issue for lighting billets).	Ard
24.11.15.	Cmdr. WHITEHEAD and HOCKNEY proceeded to Marseilles on return by S Cmdr ROBINSON and BARROWS.	Ard
25.11.15.	SCRAGG Sub Cmdr posted from establishment to warrant officers with MHOW Brigade	Ard

SERIAL NO. 304.

Confidential

War Diary

of

G.O.C. 1st Indian Cavalry Division

FROM 1st December 1915 TO 31st December 1915.

CONFIDENTIAL

CR/715/22/1/16

D.A.A.G.

Major A.F.N. Barron R.A.
S.O.D.
=
D.A.D of
1st Ind: Cav. Divⁿ

J.C. Sherwood
Lieut-Colonel,
Officer i/c Army Ordnance Corps, Records,
British Exped. Force.

10 JAN 1916

Army Form C. 2118.

WAR DIARY
or
INTELLIGENCE SUMMARY.
(Erase heading not required.)

Instructions regarding War Diaries and Intelligence Summaries are contained in F. S. Regs., Part II, and the Staff Manual respectively. Title pages will be prepared in manuscript.

Hour, Date, Place.	Summary of Events and Information.	Remarks and references to Appendices.
LONGPRÉ		
1. 12. 15.	Lieut. SHEAD. A.O.D. left for 47th Divn.	Apt 1/12
17. 12. 15.	Railhead moved to BOUTTENCOURT. Reserve of Smoke helmets, boots issued though auxbingers went by rail	Apt 17/12
23.12.15.	1850. gifts Blankets from the I.S. Fund were issued to complete new Indians with 2 blankets each	Apt 23/12

SERIAL NO. 304

Confidential

War Diary

of

G.O.C. 1st Indian Cavalry Division

FROM 1st January 1916 TO (0) 31st January 1916

Army Form C. 2118.

WAR DIARY
or
INTELLIGENCE SUMMARY.
(Erase heading not required.)

Instructions regarding War Diaries and Intelligence Summaries are contained in F. S. Regs., Part II, and the Staff Manual respectively. Title pages will be prepared in manuscript.

Hour, Date, Place.	Summary of Events and Information.	Remarks and references to Appendices.
BOUTTENCOURT.		
20. 1. 16.	Lieut C. DOUGLAS WHITE. A.O.S.H. attached A.O.D arrived from base for instruction	And roll
27. 1. 16.	1st Canadian Cavalry Brigade moved 1st Ind Car rison. They consist of:— Head Quarters Lord Strathcona's Horse Royal Canadian Dragoons A. & B Batteries. R.C.H.A 1 Signal Troop. The brigade has been used as infantry since commencement of the war and has come to this division to be modelled into cavalry.	And roll.

SERIAL NO. 304

Confidential

War Diary

of

D.A.D.O.S., 1st Indian Cavalry Division

FROM 1st March 1916 TO 31st March 1916.

Army Form C. 2118.

WAR DIARY
—or—
INTELLIGENCE SUMMARY.

Secret

Sheet 1

(Erase heading not required.)

Instructions regarding War Diaries and Intelligence Summaries are contained in F. S. Regs., Part II, and the Staff Manual respectively. Title pages will be prepared in manuscript.

Hour, Date, Place.	Summary of Events and Information.	Remarks and references to Appendices.
DARGMIES		
5-3-16	Sub Conductor T.C.R. Barrow E.O.D transferred to Mhow Brigade.	Pwl
6-3-16	Break up of Indian Cavalry Corps. 1st Indian Cav: Div'n transferred to Third Army. Fort-Garry Horse, Canadian Cav: Rgt, returns with 4 Vickers Machine Guns. 4 Lewis Guns withdrawn. Jodhpur I.S. Lancers & Jodhpur Cav: Fd. Amb: joins Division. Canadian Cavalry Brigade transferred to 2nd Ind: Cav: Div: Sub Conductor J. Scragg E.O.D transferred to India from Mhow B'de. Left for Marseilles.	Pwl
7-3-16	Signal Squadron I.C. Corps & Lahore Cavalry Cheury Sh. attached.	Pwl
8-3-16	Conductor V.N. Strickland E.O.D ⎫ holds to 1st I.C.D's No 7218 Pte Brown A.O.C ⎬ West Arc 05857 " West A.O.C ⎭	Pwl Pwl
12-3-16	Visited D.D.O.S. Third Army	Pwl
13-3-16	Conductor Strickland reports arrival & was sent to Mhow R.S. P/e Brown & Corp. reported arrival & joined up party at sh. 90.	Pwl
14-3-16	Sub Conductor T.C.R. Barrow brought in from Mhow R.S. to Headquarters.	Pwl

Army Form O. 2118.

Secret

WAR DIARY
or
INTELLIGENCE SUMMARY.
(Erase heading not required.)

Sheet 2

Instructions regarding War Diaries and Intelligence Summaries are contained in F. S. Regs., Part II, and the Staff Manual respectively. Title pages will be prepared in manuscript.

Hour, Date, Place.	Summary of Events and Information.	Remarks and references to Appendices.
DAR ET MEET (GHQ)		
14-3-16	Three New Force Armourer Sergeants reported for duty under Departmental Order No 179 and were detailed as follows:— No: 2384 Arm: Sgt. W. Rhodes A.O.C to Lucknow Bde M.G. Squadron. No: 2369 " H.F. Loft A.O.C " Mhow No: 2379 " H.E. Gaylor A.O.C " Sialkot	Rwd
18-3-16	Major Barron R.A. D.A.D.O.S. transferred to India. Division taken over by Lieut. H.S. Bigg-Wither A.O.D	Rwd
20-3-16 10	P.H (tube) Smoke Helmets issued, 1 per all ranks.	Rwd
AUXI-LE-CHATEAU 24-3-16 25-3-16	I P (tube) Helmets withdrawn from all ranks & taken into Divisional reserve. D.A.D.O.S & his office & store staff moved into Third Army Area. Office & 'dump' settled at Railhead. (AUXI-LE-CHATEAU)	Rwd
26-3-16	New Railhead opened. Visits D.D.O.S Third Army	Rwd
27-3-16	"O" Bty R.H.A transferred temporarily to 5th Division. 13th Bde's Rifle Brigade & Third Army Infantry School of Instruction attached to 1st I.C.D for Ordnance Services. Lucknow Casualty Clearing Stn & Signal Sqdn I.C.Corps transferred to 2nd I.C Div.	Rwd

H.S. Bigg-Wither Lieut. A.O.D
D.A.D.O.S
1st I.C.D 1/4/16

Gulab Singh & Sons, Calcutta.—No. 22 Army G.—5. 8-14—1,07,000.

SERIAL NO. 304.

Confidential
War Diary

O. C. D. O. & 1st Indian Cavalry Division

FROM 1st April 1916
TO 30th April 1916.

Army Form C. 2118.

Secret

WAR DIARY
or
INTELLIGENCE SUMMARY.
(Erase heading not required.)

Instructions regarding War Diaries and Intelligence Summaries are contained in F. S. Regs., Part II, and the Staff Manual respectively. Title pages will be prepared in manuscript.

Sheet 1.

Hour, Date, Place.	Summary of Events and Information.	Remarks and references to Appendices.
Auri-le-Chateau 1-4-16	Divisional Armourers shop established at Railhead.	Ro
WAIL. 2-4-16	Moved office to Divl H.Qrs at WAIL	Ro
4-4-16	"P" Smoke Helmets withdrawn from all units and replaced by "P.H." "P" Helmets returned to Divisional reserve and "H" previously held in reserve returned to Base.	Ro
8-4-16	31 Hotchkiss guns (.303) received and issued	Ro
10-4-16	3000 Steel Helmets allotted to Division & wired for. "P.H." Smoke Helmets ordered to form Divl reserve and for "P" to be returned (except 2500 for drill purposes). "P.H." Helmets wired for.	Ro
17-4-16	Divisional Bootmakers shop opened. 27 Hotchkiss guns (.303) received & issued.	Ro
23-4-16	760 Antigas Goggles ordered to form Divisional reserve & wired for.	Ro
25-4-16	13-Pdr equipment orders to be exchanged for 18-Pdr equipment.	Ro

Army Form C. 2118.

WAR DIARY
or
INTELLIGENCE SUMMARY.

(Erase heading not required.)   Sheet 2.

Hour, Date, Place.	Summary of Events and Information.	Remarks and references to Appendices.
YVRENCH		
27-4-16	Moved office from WAIL to YVRENCH	
28-4-16	Wires for 18 pdr equipment to relieve 13 pdr &	
29-4-16	700 Antigas Goggle relics for Divisional reserve	
	13th Batt. Rifle Brigade left area of 5th Batt.	
	Sherwood Foresters arrived	
30-4-16	Received advice that 12 18-pdr guns &	
	limbers due to arrive on 1st prox.	
		H.Q. Brigg. letter 1st A.O.D
		D.A.D.O.S
		1st Indian Cavalry Divn

SERIAL NO. 304

Confidential
War Diary
of

H.Q.R.A. 1st Indian Cavalry Division

FROM 1st July 1916 TO 31st July 1916

Army Form C. 2118.

Sent ✓

WAR DIARY
or
INTELLIGENCE SUMMARY

D.A.D.O.S.
1st Indian Cavalry Division

(Erase heading not required.)

Instructions regarding War Diaries and Intelligence Summaries are contained in F. S. Regs., Part II, and the Staff Manual respectively. Title pages will be prepared in manuscript.

Hour, Date, Place.		Summary of Events and Information	Remarks and references to Appendices.
YVRENCH			
1-5-16	—	18 pdr gun wagons & limbers received and issued to "A" & "4" batteries and Div.l Am.n Column. 13 pdr equipment withdrawn	Pw
WAIL			
6-5-16	—	Head office to Wail	Pw
7-5-16	—	10,500 "P.H." tube smoke helmets received to replace the P.H. helmets on Divisional reserve at the rate of 1 per all ranks.	Pw
LE CAUROY			
9-5-16	—	Moved office to Le Cauroy	Pw
10-5-16	—	Moved Dump & Workshops to Le Cauroy. Rations changed from Auxi-le-Château to Frevent.	Pw
11-5-16	—	50 gun rds & 25 ammunition sets of Hotchkiss packsaddlery received and issued	Pw
		C.I.O.M. inspected 18 pdr equipt with C.R.A.	Pw
16-5-16	—	30 gun & 15 ammn sets Hotchkiss packsaddlery received and issued	Pw

Army Form C. 2118.

WAR DIARY
or
INTELLIGENCE SUMMARY.

(Erase heading not required.) Sheet 2

Instructions regarding War Diaries and Intelligence Summaries are contained in F. S. Regs., Part II, and the Staff Manual respectively. Title pages will be prepared in manuscript.

Hour, Date, Place.	Summary of Events and Information	Remarks and references to Appendices.
18.5.16	H. Qrs. R.H.A. Bde. "A" & "U" batteries and gun section Div¹ Amm⁰ Column left to join 51st Division	
19.5.16	Gun section Ammunition Park ordered to join XVII Corps.	
20.5.16	Reserve Park joined Division	
22.5.16	Two remaining Armourer Staff Sergeants called in from Brigades. Armourers shop enlarged. Native armourers 1 per brigade, called in for instruction in the Hotchkiss gun	
23.5.16	Order received from D.D.O.S. for Reserve Park to be administered by O.O. 2 Army Troop Res.	
26.5.16	Vickers Machine Guns called in to Armourers Shop for inspection at the rate of 1 per M.G. Squadron per day the three M.G. Squadron Armourer Sergeants (New force) called in for instruction & inspection (2 days).	

H. R. W. Lew Capt. A.O.D
D.A.D.O.S
(5) Indian Cavalry Division

Army Form C. 2118.

D.A.D.O.S.
18 Indian Cavalry Division

WAR DIARY
or
INTELLIGENCE SUMMARY.
(Erase heading not required.)

DUPLICATE

Instructions regarding War Diaries and Intelligence Summaries are contained in F. S. Regs., Part II, and the Staff Manual respectively. Title pages will be prepared in manuscript.

Hour, Date, Place.	Summary of Events and Information	Remarks and references to Appendices.

YPRENCH
1-5-16

WAIL
6-5-16
7-5-16

LE CAUROY
9-5-16
10-5-16
11-5-16
15-5-16

Army Form C. 2118.

WAR DIARY

or

INTELLIGENCE SUMMARY.

(Erase heading not required.)

Instructions regarding War Diaries and Intelligence Summaries are contained in F. S. Regs., Part II, and the Staff Manual respectively. Title pages will be prepared in manuscript.

Hour, Date, Place.	Summary of Events and Information	Remarks and references to Appendices.

SERIAL NO. 304.

Confidential
War Diary
of

D.A.D.O.S., 1st Indian Cavalry Division.

FROM 1st June 1916 TO 30th June 1916.

Army Form C. 2118.

WAR DIARY
or
INTELLIGENCE SUMMARY.
(Erase heading not required.)

D.A.D.O.S.
1st Indian Cavalry Division

Instructions regarding War Diaries and Intelligence Summaries are contained in F. S. Regs., Part II, and the Staff Manual respectively. Title pages will be prepared in manuscript.

Hour, Date, Place.	Summary of Events and Information	Remarks and references to Appendices.
LE CAUROY		
3-6-16	Original allotment of 2965 steel helmets complete	Rx
27-6-16	1903 steel helmets withdrawn & issued to 37½ & 35½ Division under orders from 3rd Army.	Rx
30-6-16	"A", "Q" & "U" Bde. Train section of D.A.C. & D.A.P. of R.H.A. Res. H.Qrs returned to the Division. Moved office & dump to Doullens. Both consignment of respirators for the Vickers & Hotchkiss M.G. detachment 1 & 2 of which received & issued.	
		W.T. Whitier Capt. A.P.D. D.A.D.O.S. 1st Indian Cavalry Division

SERIAL NO. 304.

Confidential

War Diary

of

D.A.D.O.S. 1st Indian Cavalry Division.

FROM 1st July 1916 TO 31st July 1916.

Secret

Army Form C. 2118.

WAR DIARY for July

of D.A.D.O.S
1st Indian Cavalry Division

INTELLIGENCE SUMMARY.

(Erase heading not required.)

Instructions regarding War Diaries and Intelligence Summaries are contained in F. S. Regs., Part II, and the Staff Manual respectively. Title pages will be prepared in manuscript.

Hour, Date, Place.		Summary of Events and Information	Remarks and references to Appendices.
AUXI-LE-CHATEAU			
2-7-16	----	Moved office & 'Dump' in here to-day	Rw
9-7-16	----	6 Sets of experimental packsaddlery for Hotchkiss	Rw
		Gun received & issued 2 to each Brigade for trial.	
17-7-16	----	"U" B'y R.H.A left to join 5th Division	Rw
VILLERS-CHATEL			
19-7-16	----	Moved office here to-day, Dump to Tinques (Railhead)	Rw
21-7-16	----	500 Steel helmets received & issued to working parties in trenches	Rw
22-7-16	----	Base changed from Havre to Calais	Rw
27-7-16	----	Moved 'Dump' in to Villers-Chatel leaving greater portion of reserve of smoke helmets at R'head.	Rw
30-7-16	----	First consignment received from Calais 1 Hotchkiss Gun for 19th Lancers to replace "U" received and issued.	Rw

H.T. (Phillip) Willis Capt A.O.D
D.A.D.O.S
1st I.C.D

DADOS
1st Indian Cavalry Divn
Aug 1916

404

VICKERS-CHATEL

4.8.16	---- 500 Steel helmets received & issued.
8.8.16	---- 1000 steel helmets received & issued
9.8.16	---- LUCKNOW Cav Bde moved into VIIIth Corps area. After consultation with A.D.O.S. VIIth Corps decided to continue to supply them from this Divion utilizing the supply lorries carrying Indian rations as far as possible
11.8.16	---- 11 Stewart clipping machines received from Base under authority DOS/OSB/1/1738 Issued to A.D.V.S. for manage ears
12.8.16	---- 8 steel boots and 4 special wagons were in authority DOS O&B 2/2792 d/10.8.16 for Field Squadron R.E.
18.8.16	---- DDOS 3rd Army mems MO/30/H9 advising allotment of Hotchkiss guns to complete to this Squadron received. Wired Bde for 30 guns and necessary harsaddlery getting authority DOS/OSB 1/3560/15 d/ 11.8.16.
22.8.16	20 Hotchkiss guns and Hucksaddlery received
24.8.16	24 Hotchkiss guns and Hucksaddlery with issued received (20 gun set. 210 ammunition set.)
25.8.16	20 " " " "
29.8.	16 16 " " " "

Divn completed up to 10-4 gun per Squadron - 160 guns all 4 Special boat harsaddlery and issued 10 Field Squadron A&B Coh. AOD 22/16

Secret

Army Form C. 2118.

WAR DIARY

of

D.A.D.O.S 1st Indian Cavalry Division

INTELLIGENCE SUMMARY.

(Erase heading not required.)

Instructions regarding War Diaries and Intelligence Summaries are contained in F. S. Regs., Part II, and the Staff Manual respectively. Title pages will be prepared in manuscript.

Hour, Date, Place.	Summary of Events and Information	Remarks and references to Appendices.
VILLERS-CHATEL		
4-8-16	500 steel helmets received and issued	RW
8-8-16	1000 steel helmets received and issued.	RW
9-8-16	Lucknow Cav: Bde moved in to VIIth Corps area. After consultation with A.D.O.S. VIIth Corps decided to continue to supply them from this Division utilising the supply lorries carrying Indian rations as far as possible.	RW
11-8-16	11 Stewart clipping machines received from Base under authority D.O.S./O.S./B./1/2738 & issued to A.D.V.S. for Horse cases.	RW
12-8-16	8 steel boats and 4 special wagons wired for Field Squadron R.E. O.E.B 2/1792 of 10-8-16	RW
18-8-16	D.D.O.S. 3rd Army memo No O/30/49 advising allotment of Hotchkiss guns to complete to 4 per Squadron received. Wired Base for 80 guns and necessary packsaddlery quoting authority D.O.S./S.B 1/2566/5 of 11-8-16	RW
22-8-16	20 Hotchkiss guns and packsaddlery (20 gun eds & 10 ammunition eds) received and issued.	RW
24-8-16	24 Hotchkiss guns and packsaddlery sets received and issued. also 15 Simpero sinks	RW
25-8-16	20 Hotchkiss guns and packsaddlery sets received and issued.	RW
29-8-16	16 " " " " " " Division completed up to 4 guns per Squadron = 160 guns in all. 4 Special boat wagons received and issued to Field Squadron.	RW

H.J. Rawlinson Capt A.D 2/9/16

SERIAL NO. 304

Confidential

War Diary

of

A.A.D.O.S., 1st Indian Cavalry Division

FROM 1st September, 1916 TO 30th September, 1916

Army Form C. 2118.

WAR DIARY
for Sept/16
INTELLIGENCE SUMMARY.

A.A.D.O.S.
(1st Indian Cavalry Division.)

(Erase heading not required.)

Instructions regarding War Diaries and Intelligence Summaries are contained in F. S. Regs., Part II, and the Staff Manual respectively. Title pages will be prepared in manuscript.

Hour, Date, Place.	Summary of Events and Information	Remarks and references to Appendices.
VILLERS CHATEL		
1-9-16	550 Steel Helmets received	Nil
2-9-16	Auxiliary Horse Transport Co. transferred to O.O. 2nd Army Troops No. 1.	Nil
3-9-16	Moved office to new D.H.Q at Frohen-le-Grand. Dump	Nil
Frohen-le-Grand	to Auxi-le-Chateau	
St Ricquier		
4-9-16	Moved office to new D.H.Q at St Ricquier. Railhead closed	Nil
	at Thiepval opened at St Ricquier.	
5-9-16	Bulk demand for 21 Box Respirators for Emergency Parties.	Nil
	550 steel helmets received on 1-9-16 issued. Further 138	
	steel helmets received and issued	
7-9-16	5900 steel helmets allotted	Nil
8-9-16	Base changed from Calais to Havre	Nil
9-9-16	R.H.A. Bde rejoined.	Nil
11-9-16	Office moved to new D.H.Q at Doullens : commenced	Nil
	moving Dump to Alloyville. R'head closed St Ricquier opened Bouquemaison	
Doullens	Auxiliary Horse Transport Co. rejoined Div.	
12-9-16	Gun spares carried by Divl Ammn Park transferred to	Nil
	Auxiliary H.T. Co.	
Alloyville		
13-9-16	Moved office to new D.H.Q at Alloyville	Nil
	Formation of Divl Limbered Train of 59 Limbered G.S. waggons.	
14-9-16	Railhead closed Bouquemaison opened Freschencourt.	Nil
	5900 Steel helmets received 3AM issued 7AM.	

Army Form C. 2118.

D.A.D.O.S.
Sheet 2

WAR DIARY
for Sept 1916
INTELLIGENCE SUMMARY
(Erase heading not required.)

Instructions regarding War Diaries and Intelligence Summaries are contained in F.S. Regs., Part II, and the Staff Manual respectively. Title pages will be prepared in manuscript.

Hour, Date, Place.	Summary of Events and Information	Remarks and references to Appendices.
15-9-16	Railhead closed Frechencourt, opened Corbie. Division moved to bivouac north of Morlancourt leaving its "B" echelon and limbered Train at Querrieu. "U" B'y rejoined. Priority wire sent for 2 dial sights, 1 limbered wagon, 12 aiming posts & 12 siege lamps to make up the deficiencies.	
16-9-16 Albert	Railhead closed Corbie, Opened Albert. Moved office & dump to Albert.	Nil
18-9-16	1400 Steel helmets received & issued.	Nil
19-9-16	Received & issued stores demanded & checked.	Nil Nil
20-9-16	1400 Steel helmets received & issued on priority wire to complete to 1 per all ranks excluding Sikhs who refuse to wear them. Balance handed over to D.A.D.O.S. 41st Division.	Nil
21-9-16	3000 P.H.G. helmets received. House Base closed for clothing. Decided by Cav: Corps that gun parts should still be demanded by Div. Amm. Park although actually carried by Aux. H.T.C's.	Nil
22-9-16	P.H.G. helmets issued 1000 to each B'de.	Nil
23-9-16	Further 1000 P.H.G. helmets received from Base. Rouen Base opened for Clothing. 1000 P.H.G helmets issued to Indian B'de. as the B'de is to advance tomorrow with trench stores.	Nil Nil
26-9-16	Wire for Hotchkiss Gun demanded on 22nd received and issued. Hotchkiss Gun for 6th Cavalry to replace	Nil
27-9-16	Railhead closed Albert, opened Corbie. Division commenced 4 days' march to Ligescourt area direct from Albert to Ligescourt. Decided to move dump instead of following Div'n.	Nil Nil

Army Form C. 2118.

WAR DIARY
for Sept. /16
INTELLIGENCE SUMMARY.

D.A.D.O.S

Sheet 3

(Erase heading not required.)

Instructions regarding War Diaries and Intelligence Summaries are contained in F. S. Regs., Part II, and the Staff Manual respectively. Title pages will be prepared in manuscript.

Hour, Date, Place.		Summary of Events and Information	Remarks and references to Appendices.
28.9.16	---	Spare gun parts transferred back to Div.l Amm.n Park from A.4.T.C.l Tents and French shelters returned to A.D.O.S. Cav.Corps at Daours. Div.l Limbered Train returned to 10th Reserve Park.	Nil.
Ailly-le-Haut-Clocher 29.9.16	---	Railhead closed Corbie opened St Riquier. Moved office to Ailly-le-Haut-Clocher. Wired for "limbers" Q.F. 18 pdr. carriage for "Q" B.y R.H.A. to replace one destroyed through accidental explosion of cordite.	Nil
Ligescourt. 30.9.16	---	Railhead closed St Riquier opened Beaurainville. Moved office to new D.H.Q at Ligescourt and dump direct from Albert to Ligescourt.	Nil.

H.C. Rigg-Withers Cpt.
D.A.D.O.S.
1st E.C.D

2/10/16

SERIAL No. 304.

Confidential
War Diary
of

D.A.D.O.S. 4th Cavalry Division (late 1st S.E. Div.)

FROM 1st October 1916
TO 30th November 3rd October 1916.

Army Form C. 2118.

WAR DIARY
INTELLIGENCE SUMMARY.

(Erase heading not required.)

Oct. 1916. D.A.D.O.S 1st Indian Cavalry Division

Instructions regarding War Diaries and Intelligence Summaries are contained in F. S. Regs., Part II, and the Staff Manual respectively. Title pages will be prepared in manuscript.

Hour, Date, Place.		Summary of Events and Information	Remarks and references to Appendices.
LIGESCOURT	1-x-16	Divisional limbered Train & Auxiliary H.T.Cs transferred to XIV Corps	
		1 Maltese Cart demands for M.V. Sect. Lucknow on Indent No 1563/EC.	
	2-x-16	1 Wagon Amm° Q.F. 18 pdr for Amm° Column wind for (244/EC.)	Rec
	4-x-16	1 Limber Q.F. 18 pdr Carriage for "Q" Bty R.H.A. received	Rec
	5-x-16	1 Maltese Cart received for M.V. Section Lucknow Regt	Rec
	6-x-16	1 Wagon Amm° Q.F. 18 pdr received for Amm° Col	Rec
		1 Wagon Amm° Q.F. 18 pdr for "U" Bty R.H.A wind for (250/EC)	Rec
		1 Wagon G.S. for 17th Lancers	
		1 Wagon Limbered G.S. fitted for M.G. Equipt Sialkote 19th) wind for	Rec
		1 Mess Cart & 1 Cask water tank for 2nd Lancers) (252/EC.)	
	9-x-16	1 Wagon Amm° Q.F. 18 pdr received for "U" Bty R.H.A	Rec
	10-x-16	1 Wagon Limbered G.S. this for M.G. Equipt Sialkote 19th) received	Rec
		1 Mess Cart) for 2nd Lancers	
		1 Cask water tank)	
	11-x-16	1 Wagon G.S. for H.Qrs R.H.A Bde wind for (262/EC.)	Rec
	12-x-16	1 Wagon Q.F. received from Abbeville for 17th Lancers	Rec
		1 2-wheeled vehicle for Wireless receiving set demanded for W.B?	
		R.H.A under G.R.O. 897	
	13-x-16	1000 Shrapnel helmets P.H.G. received	Rec
	14-x-16	1000 P.H.G helmets issued.	Rec
	15-x-16	2 Hotchkiss Guns wind for (272/EC.) 1 for 2nd Lancers 1 for 36th J.H	Rec
		15 rubber sheets Indian through Base Ord. Depot. Inter. 2 Beds)	
		900 P.H.G Smoke helmets received	Rec

Army Form C. 2118.

D.A.D.O.S
1st E.C.D

WAR DIARY
of Oct: 1916
INTELLIGENCE SUMMARY.
(Erase heading not required.)

Instructions regarding War Diaries and Intelligence Summaries are contained in F. S. Regs., Part II, and the Staff Manual respectively. Title pages will be prepared in manuscript.

Hour, Date, Place.		Summary of Events and Information	Remarks and references to Appendices.
LIGESCOURT (cont?)	16-x-16	---- 900 P.H.G. Smoke Helmets issued	Rev
	17-x-16	---- 2,600 P.H.G. Smoke Helmets received	Rev
	18-x-16	---- " " " " issued	Rev
	19-x-16	---- H:Qrs R.H.A. B/s "A" "Q" & "U" Batteries and Gun Section D.A.P transferred to 1st Cavalry Div/s.	Rev
		2 Hotchkiss Guns received for 2nd Lancers & 36th Jacob's Horse	
		1 Wagon limbered G.S. Ford for H: G: Sqdn's Ithaca (B/s wind for (293/EC.)	
	20-x-16	---- 10,000 Blankets G.S. wind for (293/EC.) on G.R.O (281/EC.)	Rev
		1270 of. 21-11-15.	
	21-x-16	---- 1 Cart water tank for 6th Inniskilling Dragoons wind for (281/EC) received	Rev
	22-x-16	---- 2,000 P.H.G. Smoke Helmets issued	Rev
		---- 2,000 P.H.G. Helmets issued	
		Sialkot Lucknow & Mhow B/s M.G. Sections transferred to XIII Corps	
		H:Qrs R.H.A B/s, 3 Batteries & Gun section D.A.P M/Qn	
		2 Limbers (Amm) Q.F. 18 for Mark II for "Q" B/y R.H.A	
		wind for (203/EC.) 16 Mules Mark I wdr D.O.S wire B/I/379	
		of. 21-x-16 & A.D.O.S Cavalry Corps OC/112 of. 22-x-16	
		Bulk wire for 2,000 Cap: machintosh	
	23-x-16	---- Reserve of smoke helmets raised to 2,500 – wdr G.H.Q. Q.O.F	Rev
		No 317/29/A of. 15-x-16 Cav.Corps COI(6 of. 17-x-16 – & Galosses	
		of 8,000 sent to Base. Been standind "UNUSED".	
	24-x-16	---- 10,000 Blankets (2nd Blanket) wind for (301/EC.) with 263 cavalry	Rev
		Authority O.M.G. G.H.Q. Q.O.F 5642/A of. 24-10-16	Rev
	25-x-16	1,900 Capes machintosh received.	Rev

Army Form C. 2118.

WAR DIARY
INTELLIGENCE SUMMARY.

Oct: 1916. D.A.D.O.S. 1st I.C.D

(3)

(Erase heading not required.)

Hour, Date, Place.	Summary of Events and Information	Remarks and references to Appendices.
LIGESCOURT (Cont⁹) 26-x-16	1 Hotchkiss Gun for 2nd Lancers wired for (291/I.C.) to replace one broken through snapping of pinion with steel. 41 Stewart-Clipping machines received & issued. 1. Q.F. 18 par. gun & carriage received for "U" B⁷ R.H.A. reconsigned from 1st Cav. Div.. Worn gun returned to Calais. 1900 Cooper machinish issued. 2 Wagon G.S. } for "Q" B⁷ R.H.A. wired for (293/I.C.) 1 Cart. machine, hand	Rec
27-x-16	2 Limbers Q.F. 18 par. Carriage Mark II received for "Q" B⁷⁴	Rec
29-x-16	Special lorries with (308/I.C.) for 9,800 Horse Rugs. Antoux Indian Cav. Corps Q 247/3 Br. [illegible] 5-x-16 Run received & issued	Rec
30-x-16	Hotchkiss Gun for 2nd Lancers received & issued	Rec

A.E. Richardson Capt.
D.A.D.O.S
1st I.C.D
31-x-16

SECRET

WAR DIARY

OF

D.A.D.O.S. 4th CAVY. DIVISION.

Nov. 1st to 30th, 1916.

Army Form C. 2118.

D.A.D.O.S
1st Indian Cavalry
Division

WAR DIARY
or
INTELLIGENCE SUMMARY.
(Erase heading not required.)

Nov 1916

Instructions regarding War Diaries and Intelligence Summaries are contained in F. S. Regs., Part II, and the Staff Manual respectively. Title pages will be prepared in manuscript.

Hour, Date, Place.	Summary of Events and Information	Remarks and references to Appendices.
ST VALERY-SUR-SOMME		
2-XI-16	Moved Office and Armourers' Shop to St Valery: Dump to Woincourt (Railhead). First consignment of horse shoes (issues for frost cogs) received.	Buy
3-XI-16	2700 Blankets (2nd blanket per man) received and issued.	Rev
4-XI-16	3500 Blankets " " "	Rev
5-XI-16	4100 Horse Rugs received & issued.	Rev
6-XI-16	2 G.S. Wagons	
	1 Cart water Tank } for "Q" Bty R.H.A.	Rev
	1 Cart water Tank for 6th Inniskilling Dragoons	
	1 Machine Cart & harness (for Winter wearing set) for "U" Bty armed received or Units instructed to take delivery	
7-XI-16	5690 Horse rugs received.	Rev
8-XI-16	1 Cart water Tank HDQ for Lucknow Cav Bde Ambce indent from 38th C.I.H. indent for (316/EC)	Rev
11-XI-16	1 Cart Officers' Mess & Cover for A.C.I.H. indent for (316/EC)	Rev
	12 Wagons Limbered M.G. for Hdsars M.G. Squadron of Brigade indent for (317/EC) on charge of Establishment from Indian (a British) authority. G.H.Q. No O/B 926 of 2-11-16	Rev
16-XI-16	Special bulk indent for 40 Sayer Straps (wire no 334/EQ) authority Cav Corps order No 62 of 15-11-16.	Rev

Army Form C. 2118.

WAR DIARY
INTELLIGENCE SUMMARY
for Nov. 1916

D.A.D.O.S 1st Indian Cavalry Div.
2nd sheet

(Erase heading not required.)

Instructions regarding War Diaries and Intelligence Summaries are contained in F. S. Regs., Part II, and the Staff Manual respectively. Title pages will be prepared in manuscript.

Hour, Date, Place.	Summary of Events and Information	Remarks and references to Appendices.
ST VALERY-SUR-SOMME		
19-XI-16	"A" B^y R.H.A transferred to IV Corps. "M" B^y R.H.A transferred to IV Army School. Wired for 1 Hotchkiss Gun for 2nd Lancers	Rw
20-XI-16	20 special mess tins for trial & report received & issued. Mhow B^{de} M.G. Squadron rejoined Division	Rw
21-XI-16	Hotchkiss Gun received for 2nd Lancers. Mhow Pioneer Battalion left to join III Corps Lucknow " " I Anzac Corps Sialkot " " XIV Corps Cav: F^d Amb^y " how B^{de} M.G. Squadron	Rw Rw
23-XI-16	1 Vickers Gun received for 17th Lancers	Rw
25-XI-16	1 Water Cart received for Lucknow Cav F^d Amb^{ce}	Rw
26-XI-16	Received notice of change of name of Division from 1st Indian Cavalry to 4th Cav: Div^s C.G.H.Q. OB/1835 of 22.11.16 Wires for 1 Cast Officers there for H.Q^{rs} R.H.A B^{de}	Rw
27-XI-16	Lucknow & Sialkot B^{de} M.G. Squadrons returned	Rw
28-XI-16	19 Chelt cultus wires for authority Q.O.S/850/A of 27.11.16	Rw
	105 Rodetor Path joined Division	Rw
	12 Wagons limbered M.G. received for Mhow B^{de} M.G. Sqn	Rw
30-XI-16	18 pdr: guns 6, carriages 6, Limbers 6, wagons ammⁿ 18 wagons Limber 18 aringed for "O" B^y R.H.A and equivalent number of 18 pdr equipment returned by "O" B^y in same trucks. Authority O.B/1342 of 18 Nov 16.	A.L. Bigg Wither Capt D.A.D.O.S 4th Cavalry Div^s 2-xi4-16

SERIAL NO. 304.

Confidential
War Diary
of

D.A.D.O.S. 4th Cavalry Division.

FROM 1st December 1916 TO 31st December 1916.

Army Form C. 2118.

WAR DIARY or **INTELLIGENCE SUMMARY.**
for Dec.
(Erase heading not required.)

D.A.D.O.S
4th Cavalry Divn

Instructions regarding War Diaries and Intelligence Summaries are contained in F. S. Regs., Part II, and the Staff Manual respectively. Title pages will be prepared in manuscript.

Hour, Date, Place.	Summary of Events and Information	Remarks and references to Appendices.
ST VALERY-SUR-SOMME		
4-12-16	14 Chaff Cutters received. 1 Mess Cart for H.Qrs R.H.A. Bde received. Wire for 2 Vickers Guns (2 Mk V Tripod mountings) & Auxiliary mountings for Sialkote Bde M.G. Sqdn & 10,000 rounds Cartridges S.A.A blank without bullet received and issued.	Rw.
6-12-16	20 Soyers stoves received. Bulk indent (Wire 361/IC.) for 5700 Blankets G.S. (third blanket for Indians) Authority D.D.O.S. G.H.Q 4698 of. 28.11.15 & A.D.O.S. Cav: Corps No CO/211 dated 1-12-16.	Rw
7-12-16	Bulk indent (wire 363/IC.) for 300 Lamps F.S. Pt /6. Authority D.O.S. O.S.A 2/6753/1 of. 1-12-16 & Cav: Corps order No 73 of. 4-12-16. 1 G.S. Wagon for Sialkote 13th Br Qr wing for	Rw
9-12-16	10 Hotchkiss Guns received. (1 p/w Regt: to shipping purposes) 2 Vickers Guns & mountings recd for Sialkote M.G. Sqdn to replace unserviceable.	Rw
11-12-16	20 Soyers stoves received, completing allotment of 40 for the Divn.	Rw
12-12-16	1 G.S. Wagon for Sialkote Bde H.Qrs received. 5700 blankets drawn from Abbeville and issue made direct to Brigade units. Balance for Divisional units, brought to dump at Woincourt for distribution.	Rw

Army Form C. 2118.

WAR DIARY or INTELLIGENCE SUMMARY.

(Erase heading not required.) Sheet No. 2.

Dec. 1916
D.A.D.O.S.
4th Cav. Divn.

Instructions regarding War Diaries and Intelligence Summaries are contained in F. S. Regs., Part II, and the Staff Manual respectively. Title pages will be prepared in manuscript.

Hour, Date, Place.		Summary of Events and Information.	Remarks and references to Appendices.
St VALERY-Sur-SOMME (cont'd)			
	13-12-16	Sialkot B'ty Pioneer Battalion left to relieve Mhow B'ty Batt'n with 1st Div'n. Lucknow B'ty 2nd Battalion left to relieve 1st Battalion with 1st Anzac Corps.	Rw.
	15-12-16	180 Lamps H.C. F'ld/16 received + issued.	Rw.
	16-12-16	1 Water cart associated by Mhow B'ty M.G. Squadron as complete turn out to Advanced H.T. Depot Abbeville, this cart became surplus on change of establishment from Indian to British.	Rw.
	17-12-16	4 Chaff cutters received	Rw.
	19-12-16	Special indent for 8 Field Forges & 1 cart anvil (vide No 4 C.D./375r) authority D. Ordnance O.S.A 6434 dt. 17-12-16. Thula No 200594 which left Havre on 15th Nov'r arrived: containing 560 lamps 12.E. 15th/16 wind for in 11th Div'n & horseshoes, oil grease etc.	Rw.
	21-12-16	Wire for 1 Limber Wagon Q.F. 13 pr M.b.E. for O Battery R.H.A. to replace the M.b.I. recently received with the m.b. of the 13 pr. equipment. Authority D.Ordnance wire B1/2027 of 21-12-16.	Rw.
	26-12-16	M.b.E. Limber Wagon for "Q" 13 pr R.H.A. received	Rw.
	30-12-16	Indents for 13 pr equipment for "A" B'ty R.H.A-6 arrive on the 8th Jan. Authority D.Ordnance O.S.B 1/1352/2 date 27-12-16.	Rw.

[signature] Capt.
D.A.D.O.S
4th Cav. Divn.

www.ingramcontent.com/pod-product-compliance
Lightning Source LLC
Chambersburg PA
CBHW081557160426
43191CB00011B/1961